# I Can Feel Your Pain:

# How to Cope With Life As An Empath

Elise Lebeau, Ph.D.

Professional Intuitive

Thanks to...

My son, Etienne, for inspiring me to be a better person so I could be a better mom.

My companion, Jonathan, for his unconditional love and support, even when I have no idea where I'm going.

My mom and dad, for doing everything they could to help me.

Bruce, who made this book possible.

And all my fairy-winged-typo-hunting editors.

Hi, I am so glad you're here!

For years, I have been looking for you. It was hard at first, because you didn't talk to anyone about your experiences. Maybe you were scared because it had been made clear to you that this is not real, that what you are is impossible.

You got the *are-you-kidding-or-crazy* look.

Having lived in silence myself, I am intimately aware of its destructive power. I doubted. I lied. I hid from the truth. I drank. I worked too much. I drowned myself in other people's problems so I would not have to face my own. I hated all of this. I hated myself.

It took me years to detangle my inner yarn balls and I was mostly alone, like you. That was the hardest part: the isolation.

So here I am, on the other side of the mountain, where it's sunny. I understand myself. I know what I need to be happy. I feel in control of my emotional life. I know other people like me.  My clients appreciate my Empath skills and every time I help someone, it makes my heart sing.

So you see, it can be done.  You're not alone anymore.

# I'm A What?

Hi! My name is Elise Lebeau. I'm a software engineer, a single mom and a professional Empath.

The first two descriptions usually go by unnoticed, but the last one always gets me a raised eyebrow and a hint of the are-you-kidding-or-crazy look. If you're an Empath, you know exactly what I mean.

To all those you gave me that look: I don't blame you. I know it sounds crazy. But my life didn't make sense until I realized the meaning of my unusual emotional experiences.

That realization was difficult because the word Empath did not exist when I was a kid. Or an adult, for that matter. Well, it did exist, but it referred to fictional characters in science-fiction TV shows or role-playing board games. Basically, it was not real. So for most of my life, I was limited to describing myself as being "weird".

Looking back on my childhood, there were subtle signs that something unusual was going with me.

Teachers, babysitters, and friends often complimented my parents on having raised such a quiet child. I remember a Friday afternoon in first grade when our teacher was sick. We knew we had to complete our schoolwork in silence, but the noise level rose steadily with excited pre-weekend chatter until an exasperated second grade teacher stumped in and ordered everyone to pipe down. As she left, she turned to me in surprise and exclaimed: "Why don't you follow Elise's example and read a book!"

I was mortified and blushed furiously under the fiery stares of my classmates. I hated when attention was drawn to me. It felt like little daggers poking at my skin, making me feel exposed and unsafe. My only recourse was to lower my gaze back to the novel I was reading and wait for the anxiety to pass.

This event is one of many examples where my demeanor was misunderstood: I was not an obedient child compliant to a teacher's request, but a helpless victim of my own internal chaos, paralyzed like a deer in headlights.

My rambunctious classmates triggered a state of near panic within me, as I scrambled to contain a wave of confusing internal sensations and emotions. Reading was a God-sent distraction that helped me ride the storm until it passed. It gave me a focus, away from myself.

After school, I would sit in the back of the car without saying a word. I looked normal on the outside, but I was completely dazed inside. The emotions of the day would play back, like watching an old movie, as I tried to process and tame my internal chaos.

When we got home, I went to my room, closed the door and did my homework. Finally, it was quiet. A perfect child.

No one knew that I was in a constant state of internal overload, not even me. We didn't even know there was a problem.

This is a common thread through the fabric of Empath lives: we don't know that something unusual is happening to us - something that other people don't feel. And because we don't know, we don't talk about it.

I have worked with thousands of Empaths in the last decade, and few of them had talked to someone about their experiences.

In fact, I was usually the first person to ever hear their real, uncensored story. Maybe because they knew I would not give them the are-you-kidding-or-crazy look.

Or if this is crazy, at least we can be crazy together.

# What is an Empath?

An Empath is a sensitive person who can

absorb the emotions of others:

We feel what they feel.

Although it sounds like an awesome super power, it's actually an exhausting reflex, especially if you don't know you're doing it, and most Empaths don't.

The path to understanding the Empath Experience is like an obstacle course: you're hitting emotional hurdles no one else can feel; you have to jump over the fact that this sounds crazy; and to cross the finish line, you must learn to control an unconscious reflex. This journey can take a lifetime.

The challenge of being an Empath is also compounded by the wide variety of our experiences. Not every Empath is the same, so it's not always easy to describe. For example, it's a myth that all Empaths are introverted and quiet. Some of us like the spotlight and shine on stage.

However, there is common ground that most of us have walked.

## Sensitivity

Being called "sensitive" is probably the first one.

As a kid, I would cringe at bright lights and loud noises. My intolerance was so bad that I wore sunglasses indoors to avoid triggering a migraine. This sensitivity can express itself in different ways, such as allergies to food or acute awareness of smells.

My own sensitivity also extended to my emotions. I remember a teenage sleepover at a friend's house where we were running around the stairwell, grabbing the post to make a sharp turn and avoid hitting the wall. I didn't see what happened because my friend was behind me, but she slipped and hit her head on the corner of a glass coffee table.

We went to the hospital and she got several stitches to close the gash on her eyebrow. As she came out of the emergency room, tears were streaming down my face. She looked at me, surprised. "I'm ok now", she said, "It doesn't hurt anymore", but I was inconsolable and could not stop crying. Puzzled, she turned to her mom and asked her why I was still crying. Her mom looked at me and ventured a guess that I was upset because she had gotten hurt, but even she seemed confused by my reaction.

I finally pulled myself together so we could head home, and later that night, when Michelle fell asleep, I quietly cried in my pillow. Long after she had stopped hurting, I was still sad for her pain.

Some Empaths are also Highly Sensitive Persons (abbreviated HSP), which is defined as people who process sensory data more deeply due to the biological nature of their nervous systems. This depth of processing underlies HSPs' greater tendency to overstimulation, emotional reactivity and empathy, and sensitivity to stimuli.

One in five people are born with a sensitive nervous system and the trait is detectable in babies who react differently to external stimulations. However, being highly sensitive is not considered socially acceptable and is often confused with mental disorders that have similar behaviors.

Dr. Elaine Aron's book, *The Highly Sensitive Person: How to Thrive When the World Overwhelms You,* documents the challenges and benefits of being an HSP as well as its beneficial purpose in society. This book is a fascinating read considering that Empaths are often a specialized form of Highly Sensitive Persons who are tuned into the emotions of others as a stimulus for their sensitivity.

## Alone Time

Another common experience for Empaths is the need to be alone, or at least withdraw from human interactions. This can express itself in a wide spectrum of behaviors, from reading a book on the bus to systematically avoiding groups of people like parties and shopping malls.

As a child, I always liked small spaces, away from the noise of human conversations, which is why I loved sitting in my bedroom closet. I would spend hours in there, curled up in my nest.

I was considered shy because I avoided making eye contact with other people. I was that quiet kid who doesn't say anything unless prompted to do so. Although I sometimes longed to meet new friends, the thought of saying hi to a group of kids was completely overwhelming. Eye contact, touch, and proximity could trigger a storm of emotional chaos within me, so I avoided it as best as I could.

That need for quiet also manifested itself rather dramatically in my body. I had severe ear infections as a child and I was practically deaf by the time I was 6.

Being deaf can look suspiciously like being quiet or distracted. My first grade teachers didn't notice anything unusual about my behavior. I just seemed to be daydreaming in class instead of paying attention. But what was really going on was that if I just looked away and didn't make eye contact with anyone, there was less internal chaos. So I retreated even farther back into my corner of quiet.

It took a while before my mom realized that I could only hear her if she was right in front of me. By then, we went to the hospital and surgery finally restored my hearing.

Looking back on it, it's clear that I was overwhelmed by something that got worse when I interacted with people. I wanted to *withdraw* from the world. Not because I hated it, but because it hurt me, unknowingly. As painful as they were, these situations allowed me to curl up in a protective cocoon, away from what ailed me.

One of my clients, Sophia, contacted me because her medical treatment and therapy could not alleviate the panic attacks she experienced in crowded places like grocery stores.

She was practically house bound, living in isolation from the world.

Sophia wondered if she might be experiencing a high level of nervousness because she was overwhelmed by everyone else's emotions, thus making her social anxiety unbearable.

Through the use of the techniques in the Empath Survival Program©, which we'll discuss later, the dreaded trips to Costco became manageable, albeit not completely comfortable.

It's important to note that being an Empath is not a disorder, but it also doesn't mean that you are not affected by mental illness.

It is critical to first address any concerns in that area by consulting a qualified health care professional to rule out a treatable mental health condition.

## Empathy

Empaths can also share a heavy dose of empathy. Our hearts bleed when watching TV ads of starving children or neglected animals. As a child, I often felt compelled to provide others with whatever they wanted. I remember having a red pen with brightly colored ink that my best friend admired. I could not resist the urge to give it to her, even though I regretted it later on. How I missed my red pen!

I gave away most of a scholarship money for college tuition to a boyfriend who wanted to pay off his car loan. And I did it again with two other guys, for completely different reasons. I was practically a boyfriend ATM even though I was a college student living off of student loans.

It's important to note that empathy and being an Empath are very different experiences. Empathy is a psychology concept where a mental stimulation, such as seeing someone who is hurt or suffering, leads to an emotional response, such as pity or compassion.

The Empath experience is the exact opposite: we first experience an emotion that we absorb from someone else, and then we mentally try to make sense of it. The trigger of empathy is cognitive, while the trigger for an Empath is emotional.

Empaths are not an external observer of another person's emotional journey: we actually go through it ourselves with them. This emotional tag-along can become extremely confusing, especially in the context of everyday relationships.

I remember being the target of a boy's animosity in high school. We had dated for a while but the relationship ended badly and he held a grudge for many years. He would flip me off behind my back, and make sarcastic comments about me when he knew I could hear him. Every time we crossed path in the hallway, a wall of hostility would hit me. No words, no eye contact, but a hot wave of hatred would push me over.

Unfortunately, I didn't understand what was happening. Why did I experience violent negative feelings towards myself as I walked past him? The emotions came first, then my mind kicked in to explain them: I must hate myself.

Without realizing it, I came up with reasons why I was so unlovable, ugly, and repulsive. It took me years to unravel that nasty bit of emotional entanglement and to finally realize I had internalized his emotions.

My self-esteem was decimated for decades by the forgotten resentment of someone who had moved on long ago.

---

## Isolation

I have vague memories of trying to talk about some of my emotional experiences as a child. I was maybe 7 or 8 years old when I told a friend at school that I was an alien. Somehow, my space parents had dropped me on earth, maybe accidentally, but I had kept some weird super powers.

This is my first memory of the infamous are-you-kidding-or-crazy look. Even as I child, I knew that what I was experiencing was weird, and being an alien was my best explanation for feelings that didn't make sense in the context of the average human experience.

I learned to keep my theory of my alien parents to myself soon enough, but this idea did spark my love story with science fiction novels, because within those fictional worlds, I had imaginary friends who knew exactly how I felt.

I remember the first seminar I organized for Empaths, at a local new-age bookstore in my hometown. I started the class with a show of hands on these two questions: 1) who suspects they are an Empath? Most of the room raised their hand. 2) Who has a friend or mentor with whom they can talk about their Empath experiences? No hands raised on that one.

Empaths are in a tricky situation: we feel things that no one else around us can feel. How can we discuss our internal struggle?

That's why I created the Empath Community back in 2007 (**http://EmpathCommunity.EliseLebeau.com**), a forum dedicated to connecting with other Empaths. Reaching out to other Empaths was such a relief, both for me and for them.

## Everyone's Confidant

An Empath's ability to experience other people's emotions makes them great listeners. We always know exactly what you mean. At a party, Empaths can be spotted sitting in the corner, listening intently to someone's tale of woes.

As I grew into my teenage years, I discovered that talking was a great outlet for me. Despite my need to be away from people when I was a child, as a teen, I was surprisingly good at conversing.

People always seemed to feel better as the conversation went on, and of course, when they felt good, I felt good too.

I noticed that something unusual would happen in those conversations: I was usually able to "guess" what they wanted to talk about. I could verbalize how they felt, even when they could not articulate their own feelings.

I remember one particular conversation with a friend who thought her boyfriend was lying to her. She wasn't able to say it clearly but she kept talking about him, as if to reassure herself. She asked if I thought he was a nice guy, if I thought I could be friends with him, if they would still date next year when we graduated.

Before I could ponder if this was a good idea, I heard myself blurt out: "Why do you think he's lying to you?" She was startled and paused for a minute while I wondered what had come over me.

But as the words sunk in, all she could do was nod sadly. She had no proof, but suspected her boyfriend was flirting with another friend of hers. She cried from relief and I felt exactly as she did every step of the way. I felt he was lying to me, I felt betrayed, I felt sad, I felt relief. As hard as it was to go on this emotional ride with her, I could feel the knot of anxiety releasing little by little. As she felt better, I felt better too.

Over the years, I had a lot more of these conversations, and suggesting solutions is a lot easier when you can *feel* the problem.

I was everyone's confidant and accidentally became addicted to solving other people's problems.

Wait... Did I just say addicted? Yes, I did! Helping others to solve their problems doesn't sound so bad, right? Helping other people feels good. It's a way to channel that emotional sensitivity into something useful.

For me, though, it became a prison, a mental cage filled with other people's unresolved problems. The *shift* from struggle to relief I experienced as I helped someone was addictive: it turned me into a problem-solving junkie.

Even in the middle of an innocent conversation about volleyball, I felt compelled to ask, "So how is it going with your brother?". I didn't know her brother but a surge of fear about him told me what to ask for her problems to tumble into my cage.

Pretty soon, all my conversations revolved around personal issues, even when the other person didn't ask for help. Helping people who have not asked for help is intrusive and inappropriate, but my self-image was defined by how many times a day I could help someone feel better. I couldn't stop myself.

In my late teens, I experienced more and more anxiety. I craved people so I could solve problems, but listening to their problems constantly left me exhausted and frustrated, as if I was filled up with unfinished business. It was never enough as I could feel under emotional issues lurking under the surface.

Fortunately, these early experiences carried me towards studying psychology in college, where I learned to tame my wild emotional skills and shape them into counseling skills.

## Finding An Appropriate Outlet

I was an avid student and would often stay after class to talk with my psychology teachers. I discovered the need for strong boundaries and realized I had some unhealthy relationships that were based solely on my ability to alleviate emotional problems. I also learned that I had to wait until someone *asked* for help before jumping into a deep conversation.

These formative years helped me re-structure my mental space and cured my addiction to solving other people's problems. I managed to control my urge to help.

Psychology provided a socially acceptable outlet for my unusual emotional skills. It was such a relief to be able to talk about it, even if only indirectly. I couldn't be fully honest about everything I felt, but being able to express even some of it was a great improvement.

Why couldn't I say everything I was feeling?  Well, I had to be careful not to freak out my clients. Although some people were relieved and grateful that I could perceive and articulate their innermost feelings, others were terrified. The words "How can you know that about me?" were my cue that I had said too much. I learned to keep quiet about some of my insights.

Unfortunately, as much as I could control my urge to help, I was unable to control my reflex to *feel*. As soon as I touched or looked at people, their feelings flooded into me like a wave of liquid emotions, sometimes tumultuous, like rage and frustration, or smothering, like depression. I was forced to board this unavoidable roller coaster day after day. Once it started, I couldn't get out.

By the end of my Bachelor's degree, I was practically a recluse. Going to parties was exhausting, as I flowed from one powerful feeling to the next. Talking to friends used up my self-control as I restrained myself from saying what I felt from them. I was completely exhausted by the time I turned 25 years old. I battled migraines and nightmares, slowly withdrawing from the world.

Like a robot, I continued in psychology, pursuing a Ph.D. so I could work as a therapist. I finished my classwork and started my internships. I was well into my third year when I hit a wall: I was unable to write my thesis. Complete writer's block.

Although I forced myself to write sentences, I knew my soulless string of citations and quoted studies was not dissertation material. I felt so empty that even words were meaningless.

It's funny how sometimes you don't realize you're going the wrong way until life yanks you out of it.

That's exactly what happened to me when I took a sabbatical from my Ph.D. and spent 3 months away from psychology. When my time was up, I knew I couldn't go back. For the first time in years, I wasn't tired! Whoohooo! But wait, what happened? Some kind of mysterious tonic in the water supply?

I spent my time off working on house renovations for a friend who didn't mind an inexperienced, but free, contractor. I didn't interact with people at all during that time.

I was alone all day long, and when I did talk to people, it had nothing to do with their personal problems. I just needed more nails. My every day interactions were blissfully stripped of emotional triggers.

This was my first light bulb moment: people were somehow the source of my exhaustion. Although I didn't really understand why, it was easy enough to fix: I made a sharp career turn into software engineering, working with computers instead of humans.

The next 5 years were almost normal. I blitzed through a Masters Degree, became an engineer, and enjoyed a successful career solving logic problems. I met my future husband at work, we got married, and then boom: everything changed overnight.

## Let's Meet Some Real Empaths

Sometimes when talking about Empaths, it can feel as though we're discussing a mythical creature: we can get a glimpse of it through the trees but never come close enough to get a good sense of what it looks like.

And yet, Empaths are just regular people: they work at the coffee shop, on the school board, at the gas station, or in a civil engineering firm. They have families, attend soccer games, and make spaghetti for dinner. Some of them know what's going on with their Empath abilities, while others do not. Either way, they all end up figuring out a way to live with it.

Although I have tried to describe as many types of Empath experiences as I have encountered in my work as an Professional Intuitive, I also want to connect you to the real story of self-aware Empaths.

I find it inspiring to know that we are not alone, and, most importantly, that people like us have learned to live in harmony with their Empath skills.

# Lynn's Story

From a very early age, I could always sense things about people that weren't noticed by my siblings or family. I couldn't figure out why people said one thing but I felt another from them. When I went to school, it seemed to accelerate. I would pick up things from teachers and fellow students. It wasn't painful in any way at the time, it was just feelings that flowed through me then moved on. I picked friends based on the emotions I sensed, though at the time I wasn't aware of it.

When I started university, it seemed to kick in full force. It was like the floodgates opened and I picked up everything going around me, both positive and negative. The positive I could cope with but the negative was overwhelming. My roommate at the time was a Buddhist and she invited me to go to meditation meetings with her. I learned to meditate and learned that I could handle the negative input flowing around me and not let it affect me.

Through out my 20s, I continued to meditate faithfully twice a day, and looking back, this practice was what kept me grounded and helped me to control my Empath skills.

By the time I married, I had slowly gotten away from meditating and while I was pregnant with my son, it really hit me. As the years went by, I noticed that if I slacked on meditating, I would get overwhelmed by the emotions I sensed from others.

Eventually, it got to the point where the only relief I felt was during meditation, but the effects would wear off in a few hours instead of lasting all day.

By then I was pregnant with my daughter. I talked to my doctor who said it was probably due to hormonal changes. But, I felt it went deeper than that. I went back to work shortly after my daughter was born, and things continued to get worse. I worked in child protection and began finding I couldn't cope with the negative feelings I was being bombarded with.

My doctor chalked it up to postpartum depression, and again I didn't feel that was the problem. I took a leave from work and found myself turning into a hermit. I could function perfectly within my home and with my immediate family but would fall apart if I had to be in large groups.

I continued to try to meditate but I was often too overwhelmed to get into that quiet place needed to effectively meditate.

So I started looking online for help. I came across the concept of Highly Sensitive Person (HSP) and found I had some of those qualities. But I couldn't find much information on how to cope with it. One day I landed on an article written by Judith Orloff and found the word "Empath". It described exactly what I was going through! So I started to Google it, and Elise's Empath Community came up. I read the Empath Survival Program online and was impressed. I started to practice the techniques and started meditating again twice a day.

This combination provided instant relief, but only if I kept at it. If I slacked for a few days, I was overwhelmed again. If I wanted to be productive and cope with my Empath skills, I found I had to commit to working a program. My outlook on life began to change the more I learned to cope and I found life to be richer, more well-rounded and something to be thankful for.

There are days where it can still be a struggle, but those are few and far between. Being an Empath is like entering a foreign land; I look at it as an adventure. You have to be willing to leave the city of your comfort and step into your inner world. What you discover is wonderful: it is yourself.

## Sandy's Story

I knew as a child that I was "different", but I didn't have a name for that difference. I couldn't quite put my finger on it. I was different, but in what way? I was sensitive to other people's emotions but I thought that was normal. I would meet people and instantly know that person; who they were and what made them tick and yet I had no idea how this worked. Nor did I realize that it was unusual.

I thought everyone was like me.

I easily connected with animals. I knew what they were thinking and I could feel what they felt. I still remember my mother taking me to the Winnipeg zoo when I was 2 or 3 years old. I desperately wanted to go and see the animals. It was an hour drive from where we lived at the time. According to my mother, we entered the zoo and I immediately lost it. I ran to the first cage, which housed a wolf, and I began to cry. I insisted that the wolf was desperately unhappy and longed to be free. I shook the cage door and yelled that it needed to be opened right away.

I think we lasted another 15 minutes at that zoo. My mother finally gave up after chasing me from cage to cage, as I itemized what each animal was feeling. I insisted that these animals needed to be set free. Much to my dismay, I was unable to help them. Instead my mother was forced to scoop up her hysterical daughter and whisk me out of there.

Throughout my teen years, I struggled. Crowds were the worst. To survive walking through a crowded area, I pictured myself floating just above the mass of people. I would mingle with them from the knees down but the rest of my body would be above in the clear air. From this imaginary, elevated vantage point, I could breathe and survive the outing.

It wasn't until I was in my mid-forties that I found out there was a name for what I was experiencing. After a discussion with a friend, he suggested that I was an Empath. I had never heard that term so I looked it up online. The first site I found detailed the traits of an Empath. I was stunned: it was as if someone had written the article about me.

I joined the Empath Community. At first I was resistant. I read a bunch of posts, knew it was me to a "t", and yet I still couldn't immediately accept it. Within the next six months I realized I couldn't ignore it any longer. I began to participate more on the Empath Community. I posted. I shared. I learned. I gradually accepted and embraced who I was.

It all made sense. My life finally made sense. I had a whole year of "ah ha" moments as I explored all things Empath.

I now understand the dynamics of my interpersonal relationships. I understand that when I attend a funeral, I have to bring Kleenex whether I know the deceased or not. The overwhelming grief that invariably bubbles out of my tear ducts is not always my own. If someone around me feels a strong emotion, I will feel it too. They don't even have to verbalize it; I will feel it regardless. I've also learned that I can wash that feeling out of my body and out my feet into the ground.

I've learned to discern my own emotions from those of others around me. I can now control what I feel and that is very liberating. Knowing who and what I am is priceless and has given me control of my life and myself. Being an Empath has turned out to be something to be embraced and appreciated. I don't think I'd trade that for anything!

## Tony's Story

About 6 years ago, I realized that my own sensitive nature was making life unbearable: I began taking time off from work because I found myself exhausted by the moods of the people around me. I felt weak and needy every day; I had a hard time deciding whether to go to my doctor and ask for antidepressants (which had done a great job before at lifting my mood and calming me – but which couldn't seem to switch off this emotional noise from other people) or try to find a new and better solution on my own.

So I went on the Internet – that great unregulated mess of information that was just as chaotic and undependable as my own life was becoming! – hoping for a clue as to why other people's emotions seemed to get inside me and bounce around in there for days at a time. That's where I found not just clues but whole online communities of people just like me!

I soon discovered that everyone had their own special definition of what being an Empath meant; I was a professional person whose life had swung out of balance, and was looking for straightforward answers on how to get on with my day without drowning in the emotions of others, but many other Empaths saw their empathy as an extension of their spiritual lives, or of their interest in paranormal phenomena. They couldn't imagine talking about it except in that context.

This was the opposite of what I wanted! I wanted to feel normal again, not to get involved in something that would make me feel even weirder and more different from all the people around me. I had to decide whether to keep sifting through all this stuff in the hope that it might yield me some answers, or call it quits and accept that I was probably never going to get useful answers from the strangers anyway.

I kept delving – immersing myself in material that was a bizarre blend of new-age spirituality and pop-psychology. Eventually, I found Elise Lebeau's material on Empaths; she carefully described Empath experiences that any Empaths could identify with, regardless of their religion or cultural background. She also offered exercises that gave immediate feedback on whether they were working or not – rather than asking that I trust in unseen spiritual forces. Her material was universal and simple, instead of esoteric and mystical - exactly what I was hoping for.

Even such a straightforward and sensible approach to empathy still had the problem that calling myself an Empaths seemed... fantastical. I worried that I was guilty of arrogance or spiritual delusion – to presume that I could share in other people's inner lives seemed more like vanity on my part.

Part of me wanted to cut ties with this weird world that I had become a part of, but the exercises worked... They really worked! And so I stuck with it, practicing the exercises every single day, going out for walks through crowds at lunch time (previously impossible for me) and exploring that distinction between just observing the people I passed by and actually merging with people through my Empath skills.

Over the course of about 3 months I found that regardless of whether I really believed that I was an Empath or not, the exercises were working and so were useful. I was seeing a big shift in the way I felt and was able to feel "grounded" in myself in a way that I never really had before.

When I meet Empaths now, I often see in them the person I used to be: off balance, easily distracted or agitated, like they're floating around outside themselves rather than grounded in their own beings. Getting control over my Empath skills has allowed me to find a new balance: I can enjoy the awareness and insight into situations and people that empathy brings, but turn down the noise of other people's emotions so that it no longer exhausts me.

## Amaya's Story

I feel like I was born with my Empath abilities switched on, rather than having them develop later in life. Although I didn't realize that I was different from everyone else in that way, I always knew I could feel other people's "stuff". In my late teens, though, there was a moment when I started freaking out about my Empath abilities because I had become so sensitive that I began to wake up immediately, even from deep sleep, whenever someone wanted to talk to me.

During that time of my life, I hung around with lots of people who did lots of drugs. A certain sub-set of the more hippy of the bunch was involved with learning about new-age spirituality, so although I didn't really talk about my Empath experiences, I ended up reading a lot about it. This was before the Internet existed, so I was a regular at the local new-age bookstore, and I found a lot of solace that such a place existed, and that I could learn so much from the books they had on hand.

The biggest struggle for me was that there was so much information out there. I didn't know where to start in trying to understand the world and how I fit into it.

I initially studied shamanism, and came upon the term "Empath" only after a thorough study of Wicca, Buddhism, Zen, Deepak Chopra, aliens, ascension, astrology, numerology, palmistry, and tarot.

In the absence of a comprehensive guide like the Empath Survival Program©, I learned a patchwork of things over the years that helped me cope.

The best thing that ever happened to me was learning a trick to shut off my Empath abilities which I found in a book about urban shamanism: a mudra or special positioning of the hands and fingers, where I connect my thumb and my index finger on both hands and interlock the rings they form. I only use it as an emergency measure when I am overwhelmed with others' emotions, and I figured out how to use it while I sleep so I don't get woken up anymore.

Otherwise, I learned to cope with my Empath sensitivities by applying mindfulness and trying to proactively recognize what's going on with each person I'm around. For example, when I get on a bus, I look around and recognize, "That woman is upset about her child. That man is on his way to something he believes will be unpleasant. That girl is newly in love. That woman is thinking about her bills." Or whatever other information is in the bus that I can't block out.

I also try to leave as much physical space as possible between me and a person experiencing strong negative emotions.

Because my gift also works at a distance, I do the same thing with the people in my life when I can't figure out where an emotion I'm feeling is coming from.

I call up a feeling of them, using a mental picture of their face or a memory of how I feel when I'm with them, and then "listen" to their current emotional state.

A big Empath breakthrough was when I gave myself permission to simply cut people out of my life that were prone to having lots of negative emotions. Now, if a person doesn't feel good to me, I don't bother with them. If it's a co-worker, I'll be polite, of course, but I will actively seek to be moved or reassigned, or I'll just start looking for a new job.

Life is too short to spend it with miserable people.

Breakups have been very difficult for me, especially one that was very negative, because I could feel everything I was feeling plus everything he was feeling. I employed my emergency measure often during that time. I also tend to take a lot of time between relationships to let the feelings of one cool off completely before starting another.

I believe that being an Empath is like most personality traits: it's a combination of genetics and environment. I think that most Empaths experience some kind of environmental trigger that switches it on, while also being more genetically prone to it. For my brother and I, that trigger came early in the form of parents that are emotionally volatile. In our case, our gifts were nurtured by a stable, long-standing group of neighborhood kids that were also Empaths. We were very lucky in that way.

One of the best parts of being an Empath has been in realizing that all people are much more similar than they are different. Everyone has the same hopes and fears, irritations and ego-dramas, and everyone thinks they're *totally alone* in how they feel.

I try to remember this when I'm the one feeling totally alone.

# Empath Awakening

Although it's not common to all Empaths, many of my clients relate having an *awakening*, a defining moment when their dormant skills jumped to the surface of their consciousness and demanded attention.

My personal awakening is easy to remember: it happened while I was pregnant with my son in 2003. My protective bubble burst open and unleashed an emotional hurricane. As if my years as an engineer had been a short nap before waking to even more powerful Empath experiences.

It was not pretty. I had no control over the internal storm I was experiencing. The feelings of everyone around me, including neighbors, coworkers, and complete strangers in the street came crashing down on me. It was chaotic and undeniable.

This was where I became concerned for my mental health. Having studied in psychology, I knew I was having symptoms of mental illness: confusion, insomnia, anxiety, random mood swings, believing impossible things. So I went into therapy for several months.

This was probably a life-saving event for me: my therapist didn't think I was crazy. She was intuitive herself and was comfortable with the idea that we can pick up "information" from other people. And since she was a licensed professional, I was inclined to believe her. It was an uphill battle, though. I took anti-anxiety medications for several months to help manage the fear and emotional turmoil I was experiencing, but as I talked to my therapist about my day-to-day experiences, without getting the are-you-kidding-or-crazy look, I began to heal.

This was a turning point for me: a life long sigh of relief. It was during this period that I decided to find a way to manage my *Empath side effects*, as I would come to call them. That's now the Empath Survival Program© was born, aptly named because I felt it had saved my emotional sanity.

The techniques in the Empath Survival Program© came to me over the course of two years through a lot of research. I scoured the Internet for suggestions on how reign in wild "spiritual skills", which was the closest description I had at the time to what I was experiencing as an Empath.

I tried hundreds of tools like grounding, shielding, white light bubbles, meditation, yoga, fasting, spiritual retreats, psychic readings, salt baths, crystals, mudras, and so many more that I can't even remember. If it helped, I documented how I was using it. If it didn't, I moved on.

This research led me to write about my Empath experience online. Having struggled to find bits of useful information, I wanted to make it more easily accessible for others who were struggling with Empath Side Effects as I had.

Writing about my experiences as an Empath started with an article published in 2005 where I used this word to describe something *real*. Not fantasy, not science fiction, not crazy. It quickly climbed to the top of the Internet search results for the phrase "are empaths real" and it's been there ever since. As a result, I started being contacted by other people who were having the same experiences I was.

I was quickly overwhelmed by the emails of people who desperately needed help. I had a young child at home and was working full time as a software engineer. My time was stretched as far as it could go. Still, I spent hours in the early morning and evening replying to requests with suggestions and support.

So I created the Empath Community (**http://EmpathCommunity.EliseLebeau.com**) to connect Empaths with each other.

In the beginning, I was the only member. I considered shutting it down several times. But I knew there had to be others out there who needed help and were seeking this connection as badly as I did. Over time, it became more visible and it's been a thriving circle of friends since then.

The most common post from new members is one filled with wonder that they are not alone. You can almost hear their sigh of relief.

But instead of spending hours replying to emails, I was now replying to forum discussions on the Empath Community, explaining over and over again how to manage wild Empath skills. It finally occurred to me to publish the Empath Survival Program© online as a self-help tool. That made a huge difference in my ability to help other Empaths on a much larger scale: they could just try the techniques and get instant relief.

By that time, through the use of the techniques that I had learned and written about, I was able to obliterate all the down sides of being an Empath from my everyday life: no more feeling exhausted, anxious in crowds, or crushed by other people's moods. I got my head above water and could finally enjoy my well-developed Empath skills.

# Impaired Empaths

My own life has taught me that there are two sides to the Empath experience: the gift of sensing other people's emotions and the curse of being overwhelmed by them.

I refer to Empaths who are overrun by side effects in everyday life as **Impaired Empaths.** Keep in mind that this is a temporary state of being. You can learn techniques to resolve these issues, which we'll discuss in the chapter on the Empath Survival Program©.

## Are you an Impaired Empath?

These are the most *common* problems encountered by Impaired Empaths.

- **Feeling drained or tired when interacting with people**. Empaths have different tolerance level for human interactions. Some feel tired after dozens of interactions, like a doctor who sees patients all day, while others are drained by an evening with a friend that involves eye contact, physical touch, and discussing a troubled marriage. This side effect can vary from needing a simple nap to chronic fatigue syndrome.

- **Being overwhelmed in large groups**. This side effect can be described as being shy or anxious around people. The sheer quantity of emotions flying around can trigger the need to withdraw or leave you feeling unsafe and exposed. I was considered anti-social in college because I didn't enjoy going to parties, but to me it felt like being tickled: it's fun at the beginning but becomes uncomfortable if it keeps going for a long time.

- **Having random mood swings that have nothing to do with what's happening in your life.** I was doing the dishes the first time I clearly identified this side effect. My kitchen sink had a window that opened towards my neighbor's front door. I was drying dishes one night, after my son had gone to bed, when I felt a surge of rage. I paused, startled by this powerful emotion. Why was I angry? I don't remember what I was thinking just before, but I was feeling calm and peaceful. I looked out the window as my neighbor stumbled out and kicked his recycling bin. It shot straight across his lawn towards the sidewalk. I could hear him mumble words of frustration. He paused and sighed. After a few moments, he went to get the bin and went back in the house. As he walked away, my own rage faded.

*Please note that these side effects can also be sign of a mental illness, such as bi-polar disorder. It's always best to consult a mental health care professional to rule out this possibility or receive medical treatment.*

# Balanced Empaths

Although I have mostly discussed emotional chaos, fear, and doubts, it doesn't mean that all Empaths are doomed to a life of despair. Some Empaths talk positively about their experience and have found ways to use their Empath skills productively, to help themselves and others.

I refer to the term *Balanced Empath* to describe someone who has mastered their Empath skills and is able to put their emotional sensitivity to good use, meaning that they have an appropriate outlet.

For example, Mark is a novelist who can deeply touch his readers because he is authentically connected to them. He can tune into his audience, get a sense of what inspires or intrigues them and fill his novels with emotional content that instantly resonates with them.

I have a friend who is a realtor and uses her skills to match people to a house that makes their heart sing.

Every Empath has their own way of expressing their skills. I've often talked to Balanced Empaths who consider it part of life's purpose to use their emotional skills in every day life.

Most importantly, a Balanced Empath has figured out how to detangle their personal feelings from the emotions of others, which is a crucial step towards a peaceful Empath experience. They can *modulate* their Empath skills at will.

I would like to make a distinction between a *Balanced Empath* and a *Professional Empath*. Being a Professional Empath requires a lot more skills, training, and practice than what I'm covering in this book.

Professional Empaths are able to interpret and convey complex emotional information ***accurately***. They can use this information for specific purposes, such as healing work or counseling. They have integrated their Empath skills into a career.

My transition to becoming a Professional Empath was sporadic and difficult. I had to learn to control my initial reflex to use my skills to help the people around me. An innocent conversation with a friend would inevitably turn into: "here's what you're REALLY feeling and what to do about it". The words would spill out of my mouth before I had time to evaluate if it was appropriate to say. And most of the time, it was not.

People get defensive *very* quickly if you suggest they might be attracted to their sister's husband...

After being whiplashed a few times by offended friends, I realized that it might be best for me to shut up. Almost ten years after leaving my career in psychology, I was still learning the same lesson: wait until someone *asks* for advice before trying to help them.

It's ironic that while I was trying to help those you didn't ask for it, I was unable to help those who did. Even after publishing my self-help tools like the Empath Community and the Empath Survival Program©, I was still getting numerous requests for help, which I could not answer for lack of time and energy.

Between taking care of my family and going to work, training Empaths just fell off the table.

In the end, I managed to put two and two together and started offering Professional Empath reading and training sessions.

Most people came to my web site and found everything they needed by themselves, but those who were overwhelmed, lost, or confused could talk to me directly and get help tailored to their specific circumstances.

# How does it work?

## Understanding the Empath Experience

Let's describe the process that is triggered when we absorb the emotions of someone else.

### The Trigger

Empaths are like radio receivers: our sensitive nervous systems pick up the emotional signals emitted by others.

Everyone around us is an emitter, constantly experiencing and broadcasting emotional signals.

Whenever we get *triggered*, we tune into a person's signal and pick up on their emotions; we're listening to their radio show.

These are the most common Empath Triggers:

- Proximity

- Eye Contact

- Physical Touch

- Specific People (loved ones, co-workers)

- Specific Situations (when someone is sad)

## The Wave

When you've tuned into someone else's emotional signal, their feelings create an emotional activation within you that works like an *echo*: you experience their rage, their sadness and their confusion. It becomes yours too.

## The Release

Once you've completed the connection with them, you let it go. You disconnect from their signal, the emotions flush out of you and it's over. You're back to being "just you".

## When Things Go Wrong

For Impaired Empaths, the process tends to work more like this...

1) **Everything is a Trigger**: Someone feels an emotion, usually a very strong and negative one, and you accidentally tune into his or her emotional signal. Even just looking at someone can trigger you. You have no control over when this happens. You can't help it or modulate it.

2) **The Hurricane Wave**: You are hit by a full-blast, ton-of-bricks emotional wave and experience high-intensity emotional activation. It wipes you out.

3) **No Release**.  This phase is skipped entirely. Most Impaired Empaths don't even know it's possible to tune down other people. So they keep feeling crappy long after the other person has moved on.

# Vanquishing the Impaired Empath Challenges

I worked with a lot of Impaired Empaths over the years and they tended to experience similar challenges. These issues were easy to spot since I had run into them myself so many times.

That's what inspired me write a self-help guide.

## The Empath Survival Program©

I designed the techniques in this program to help you overcome the most common side effects encountered by Empaths.

Since their initial publication on the Internet, these techniques have been successfully used by thousands of Empaths. I'm always delighted to get emails from people telling me they can see a light at the end of the tunnel, because they found a technique in this program that works for them.

**Keep in mind that this process takes time.** After all, we're trying to change a habit that you've had your entire life. Although most Empaths feel an *improvement* right away, it can take a couple of weeks to master a technique. Be kind and give yourself time to practice.

You might not need every technique in this book. My hope is that you won't feel stuck with an overwhelming list of things you "must do" but a short list of things you "can do" to help yourself in every day life.

One word of caution: our sensitivity is not other people's fault or responsibility. You can't resolve your emotional turmoil by asking others to stop having strong emotions.

The most empowering way to address our challenges is by looking *within* to find ways to manage emotional content, both internal and external.

## Challenge 1: Overwhelming Emotions

If you're experiencing a lot of Empath Side Effects, learning to modulate your own sensitivity to other people is an essential survival skill. It can change your life.

As an Empath, you might not be aware that tuning into other people's emotions is a *reflex*. Most of us do it without realizing it. However, you can learn to *filter* out this information when it's not relevant to what you're doing right now.

In fact, you already know how to filter *external emotions*. Have you lived in a home with a loud heater or creaky stairs? At first, you probably jumped every time you heard that unfamiliar noise, especially at night. But over time, your brain learned that this sound is *irrelevant* so it just ignored it. Voila! You just created a filter.

It works the same way for Empath skills. You need to tell your brain to create a filter for this specific "noise".

Keep in mind that we are **not trying to shut it down**. Being an Empath is part of who you are and blocking goes against your nature. Instead, we'll turn it down to a more comfortable level.

## Technique 1: Turn Down The Volume

1) Close your eyes and imagine a volume dial in front of you that goes from 0 to 10. This dial represents your *sensitivity* to other people's emotions. What number are you on? Most Impaired Empaths are always on 10, which means they are always tuning in to everyone around them.

Now let's put a label on this dial so your brain know which "noise" you want to filter. You can use something like "other people's emotions". Or if you're trying to modulate your sensitivity towards a specific person, put his or her name on the label.

2) Now turn the dial a *few notches down*. Can you get to 8? Do not try to get all the way down to 0. Your mind will refuse to do this, as being an Empath is in your nature. You can modulate, but you can't annihilate.

3) Take a deep breath to reboot your mind. It takes a moment for your brain to realize that things have changed.

**How do you know if it's working?**

Our criterion for success is a feeling of *relief*. Do you have a little more breathing room? Is your stomach easing up? Do you feel slightly calmer?

These seemingly small changes *add up over time*. The more you practice, the more often you will experience these moments of emotional calm.

## Practice

Practice this technique every time you feel "emotionally activated" throughout the day. In the first coupe of days, you might use this technique 20 times a day. That's ok. Each time you use it, it will "hold" longer and longer.

You'll be amazed how often you are taking on the emotions of others without realizing it. Using this technique feels great, like a weight has been lifted from your shoulders!

## QUICK TIP

*If you cannot move the dial down or it pops back up immediately, there might be a part of you that is reluctant to disconnect from other people's feelings.  You need to figure out WHY it's happening before the dial will stay down.*

*You can investigate this by asking yourself: "Why do I feel obligated to stay tuned in to others?" What would happen if you stopped? Would you feel guilty? Would you feel vulnerable?*

## In Real Life

*Most Empaths feel overrun by external emotions in certain situations or towards specific people, particularly when loved ones are involved.*

*Pamela called me to discuss feeling overwhelmed during meetings at her daughter's school. Her daughter Anna was struggling in second grade and Pamela regularly met with school staff to address the issue.*

*During the meetings, she would become anxious, feeling restless and aggressive. These reactions were out of character for her.*

Although she didn't mention it at first, I felt through my own Empath skills that the anxiety was her internal emotion, but the restlessness and the aggression were not. So I asked if anyone in these meetings was dominating the discussions. "Yes", she said right away, "Anna's teacher always looks angry and defensive".

That was the culprit: Pamela was tuning into the emotions of this teacher who felt defensive and upset. In turns, these confusing feelings made her feel anxious.

So we practiced Technique 1 during the session and she was ready for a more productive meeting. She was able to tune out the emotions of that teacher which melted away her anxiety.

## Challenge 2: Lost At Sea

If you've been drowning in other people's emotions for a long time, you might have a hard time knowing how *you* feel.

Once you can turn down your sensitivity to other people (Technique 1), you can focus on yourself again. As your inner space gets quieter, it's easier to hear how you feel and what you want. This technique is useful for "people pleasers" who have lost themselves in what other people want.

## Technique 2: Turn Up My Volume

1) Close your eyes and imagine a volume dial in front of you that goes from 0 to 10. Put a label on this dial that like "My Feelings" or "Me". This dial represents how much of your own feeling are available in your awareness.

2) Turn the dial up a few notches. Don't try to jump all the way to 10. This will likely bring up too many intense feelings that were kept quiet for many years. Be gentle and go up a little bit at a time.

3) Take a deep breath to reboot your mind. It takes a moment for your brain to realize that things have changed.

How do you feel right now? These emotions are yours. Be kind and gentle as you learn to process them.

### In Real Life

*Angela called me because she was completely lost in her own life. She had no idea where she was going, no sense of purpose. She felt paralyzed, unable to make a decision.*

*When I tuned into her, I could feel a patchwork of other people's wants. I could barely find her feelings underneath all these external emotions that she carried around with her. These feelings felt very old and went back to her childhood.*

*It's common for kids to want to please their parents. Getting their approval makes us feel loved and keeps us safe. But for an Empath, this can become part of how we see ourselves: through the eyes of others. To feel appreciated, we become whatever the other person wants until our own feelings are buried deep within, inaccessible.*

*First, we used Technique 1 to turn down the volume of other people wants.*

*Then we used Technique 2 so Angela could connect with her feelings. This combination revealed how she felt and she was unstuck.*

## Challenge 3: Drowning in the Crowd

Crowded venues can be very difficult for Empaths since *physical proximity* is a common trigger. Wandering through a shopping mall filled with people who are excited, frustrated, or worried about money can leave us feeling exhausted, as we try to process a huge amount of external emotional stimulation.

Our brain is always trying to make sense of our physical sensations, and some Empaths experience crowds like walking through a wall of gelatin. I remember coming out the Shanghai airport and being hit by a powerful sensation of heaviness. The high population density in China makes it a challenging location for Empaths.

## Technique 3: Filters and Shields

### Filters

A filter allows us to sort out other people's emotions and selectively ignore them. Technique 1 (Turn Down The Volume) is using a *filter*.

Filters are the best way to handle most situations because they require *the least amount of energy* on our part. It's a lot easier to filter or divert water, for example, than to build a watertight dam that completely blocks its flow. The same is true for energy.

### Instructions

Let's use a filter to move through crowds without getting overloaded.

1) Close your eyes and visualize the particles in your body getting more and more spaced out. They are expanding so there is more space between each atom in your body.

2) Imagine now that your own magnetic field is expanding too: it is as big as the room...as big as the building you're in...as big as the city block...How big can you get it???

3) There is so much space between the particles in your body that it's easy for other people's emotional signals to *slip past you* instead of getting caught in your energy field. It flows right through!

## Shields

Sometimes we're stuck in a toxic environment where filtering is not enough: the intensity of the emotional stimulation is so strong that we can't ignore it. This is where shields come in handy.

Shields are thick walls that we build around us to bounce off the emotions of others: they block everything from coming through. *Shields require a lot of energy to maintain.* If you use them constantly, you will feel exhausted. They should only be used as a temporary measure when filters are ineffective.

## Instructions

Here are two examples of a crowd shield. Pick the one you like best!

### *The Deflector*

- When you are walking through a crowd, imagine that you can *clear a path ahead of you,* like Moses parting the Red Sea. Instead of hitting you, other people's emotions are deflected to your left and to your right, allowing you to glide through without absorbing them.

## The Wall:

- Close your eyes and imagine thick walls around you. What kind of wall feels strong and powerful to you? Three feet deep concrete? Thick metal? Fully enclose yourself in a realistic bunker that feels safe.

If crowds make you really uncomfortable, rehearse at home first while imagining being in the troubling situation.

### In Real Life

*Sarah was struggling at the grocery store. Even just walking in the building on a weekday, the least busy time, would make her feel oppressed. She had to run through the store as quick as she could and rush home before she could feel calm again. On one particular occasion, she felt pushed back as she entered the store and had to turn around.*

*Trying to turn down the volume (Technique 1) wasn't enough. She was feeling physically overpowered and needed something more direct for this particularly challenging situation. We used a Deflector Shield so she could carve her path through the crowd without being rolled over by it.*

## Challenge 4: Empaths At Work

Chances are that you're the only Empath at the office. While a crowded workplace might be a challenging setting, you can create a safe space no matter where you work.

## Technique 4: Anchor Your Space

1) Practice Technique 1 everyday to lower your overall level of emotional activation.

2) While at home, select an object that represents feeling safe, calm, and secure. For example: a stuffed animal, a soothing crystal like rose quartz, a picture of the sea, etc.

3) Hold the selected object in your hands, while you think about being in a safe space and feeling free. Visualize your emotions running through the object.

4) Anchor it in your mind by saying out loud, "I am in a safe space," while holding your object.

5) Bring the object to work. It can be on your desk, or in your purse or pocket. Whenever you start to feel overwhelmed, touch your object and say to yourself, "I am in a safe space." Tune into the energy of your object to reconnect with a feeling of freedom and safety.

### In Real Life

Being a software engineer, I work a lot with stressed out co-workers. We're always behind schedule, and finding problems with the release at the last minute is very common.

We also work in cubicles, a dense environment that provides very little personal space.

I would often find myself "drifting" while I was at work, feeling tugged by the stress and preoccupations of the people around me, even if I had been in a good mood in the morning. I would grow irritable and defensive as the day stretched on. I felt like I was crammed in a shoebox with no breathing room.

I had a framed picture at home depicting a calm lake overlooking rugged mountains. The huge photograph was hanging on a wall in front of my meditation chairs and I noticed that I would relax instantly while just looking at it.

This was my first anchor. Although I could not bring my large frame to work, I found a smaller picture of the same scenery. Throughout the day, I would use it as an anchor to feel more space around me.

## Challenge 5: The Love Trap

These are the common problems for Empaths in their close relationships.

## Entanglement

Being an Empath can be a huge advantage in the beginning of a relationship because you can quickly connect emotionally with other people. But it can also become uncomfortable when you become so close that you are overwhelmed by their emotions.

This can lead to a tough situation where our own thoughts and emotions become entangled with someone else's to the point where we can't tell them apart. Is that yours? Is that mine?

For example, do you get grumpy when your spouse comes home from a bad day at work?

## Intensity

Even when positive, intense emotions can be overwhelming for Empaths. We need to pull back, oftentimes both emotionally and physically. For example, when my son was born, I was unable to hold him for more than a few minutes at a time. I felt crushed under the intensity of his emotions. I loved him dearly but I had to constantly take breaks from our physical contact.

## Interpretation

It's very easy for Empaths to misinterpret what they perceive from their partner. People often experience complex emotions that they can't fully explain or understand.

To make matters even more confusing, keep in mind that Empaths usually cannot differentiate between a conscious and unconscious emotion; to an Empath, they both feel the same.

So it's best to best to ask your partner how they feel instead of assuming that you know.

## Technique 5: Clear Boundaries

Empaths are very easily overrun by other people's emotions. We'll give in, be swayed, or settle for an unfair compromise because it's what the other person wants. It's important that we learn to keep our emotional space free from external influences.

Here's a technique to do this:

1) Before you start a discussion with your partner, take a moment to close your eyes and imagine a bubble around you about 2 or 3 feet from your body. This is a visual representation of the boundary to your personal space.

2) Enforce your emotional boundary with physical space:

- **Don't sit too close.** Leave space between the two of you so you can maintain your personal space.

- **Don't face your partner.** Instead, sit at an angle. If you're sitting across a table, aim your knees away from your partner's body.

3) If you start to feel confused or overwhelmed, pause for a moment and visualize your bubble back to its full size, pull back your chair or re-orient your body

### In Real Life

*Ron often struggled while trying to discuss relationship issues with his girlfriend. The conversation would start out fine but he would inevitably feel confused and end up conceding to her opinion.*

*This was really frustrating, as he would regret his decisions a few hours later. He felt like he was suddenly remembering what he really wanted, but it was too late.*

*When I tuned into Ron, I felt like he was trying really hard to be a good partner. All he wanted was for girlfriend to be happy in the relationship. And so during their discussions, he would tune into her feelings to be sure of how she felt.*

But when hit full force by her disagreement, he would collapse and change his position to reflect hers.

Once he understood his trigger, Ron was able to give himself more space and avoid merging into her feelings. By voicing his opinions more honestly, the couple was able to find more acceptable compromises to both parties.

## Challenge 6: Feeling Safe

It's quite natural to pay attention to things that might hurt us: it's a survival reflex.

However, this survival reflex can turn into a state of "hyper vigilance" where we're always on the lookout for negative emotions. We start to see them everywhere, and expect them all the time.

Feeling safe is such a powerful state of being for an Empath, but it's so difficult to achieve when we feel surrounded by a sea of threatening negative emotions.

Developing a sense of safety does not come from controlling the outside circumstances of our lives, but from nurturing positive feelings inside of our own psyche. If we can feel safe even when we sense that someone is angry, we have truly conquered this destructive pattern.

## Technique 6: Emotional Freedom Technique (EFT)

When we experience something emotionally painful, our brain creates a powerful emotional association based on the circumstances of that event.

For example, if you've been in a car accident, you might experience very strong negative emotions when listening to people talk about driving a car, even if you are not in danger right now. This emotional response is triggered by the memory of the traumatic event.

Such events can keep affecting us long after they happen because they the feelings surrounding them have not been fully processed by the brain. This emotional response is a sort of "bookmark" left by the brain to indicate that this memory is still active.

EFT is used to replace negative associations by tapping on soothing acupuncture points while making positive affirmations about the problematic situation, like we would use physical therapy to rehabilitate a muscle that has been injured. We are re-training your brain to bring up these new supportive thoughts on daily basis.

For beginners, EFT is a lot easier if you follow a protocol. Often, this is called "tapping along", a technique where you repeat the statements made by the EFT practitioner and tap where they tap.

## Where to Tap

Use your fingertips in a slow, gentle tapping motion in these locations.

1) **The karate chop.** The flat edge of your palm, opposite to your thumb.

2) **Forehead**. About 1 inch above where your eyebrows would meet.

3) **Temple**.

4) **Under the eye.**

5) **Under the nose.**

6) **Chin.**

7) **Collar Bone**. Tap below ridge of your collarbones. Spread your thumb and middle finger to reach both sides at once. Those spots are usually sore, you can point the right spot by looking for that tenderness.

8) **Under the arm**. Raise your arm slightly and use all fingers from the opposite hand to tap on an area about four inches below your armpit.

Let's try it right now with a Tap Along video on Feeling Safe: **http://www.EliseLebeau.com/eft#safe**

### In Real Life

*Isabel had started to struggle at work when her company hired a new employee who sat next to her office. She had grown more and more anxious over the last two weeks but couldn't figure out why.*

*Brian, the new employee, worked in accounts receivable and regularly had difficult conversations with clients who refused to pay their bill. He would sometimes threaten them with legal consequences.*

When I tuned into Isabel's energy, all I could sense was intense fear. I asked her if she was scared of Brian. "Not at all", she replied, "on the contrary, he's a very nice guy whenever I talk to him in the break room or when I leave at night".

Although she didn't mean to do it, Isabel was tuning into Brian's threatening emotions and experiencing them within her. She was not in any danger, but her mind had become hyper-vigilant to Brian's negative energy. As a result, she constantly felt "unsafe" around him.

We used EFT to train her mind to feel safe while she sat at her desk and her anxiety went away.

## Challenge 7: The Headless Chicken

Grounding is a critical Empath skill. It turns our attention away from other people's feelings and back towards our inner world. Without grounding, we're running in circles without *direction* or *focus*.

The opposite of grounding is being *distracted*. Empaths can be tuned others so much that they become confused about what they want and experience difficulty making decisions in their lives.

Grounding makes you aware of what YOU are feeling and leads to greater clarity about what YOU want.

# Technique 7: Grounding for Empaths

Here are some very effective grounding techniques that I use every day:

1) **Wash your hands**: Washing your hands is a discreet way of flushing out energy you might have picked up from other people. It cleans up your energy and quiets the noise of other people's feelings.

2) **Use visualization**: Imagine that you are growing roots from the bottom of your feet. Your roots keep reaching deeper in the earth. They're flexible too, so you can lift your feet and they follow you. Try it at home first then you'll be able to do it while you're grocery shopping.

3) **Eating**: This is a delicious way to stay grounded as long as you pay attention to the food you're eating! Pick a snack to bring along that you can eat when you start to feel overwhelmed.

### In Real Life

*I struggled for a while to find a grounding technique that worked for me.*

*I am not especially patient and meditations didn't help me, mostly because I would get irritated that they were not working RIGHT THIS MINUTE.*

*Visualization also did not work because I would just forget to do it...Oooops!*

*When I realized that eating a snack was an effective grounding technique for me, it was a simple fix to always carry a granola bar. I would reach out for it when I was in busy crowds, like my son's school or walking through a hospital.*

# Under the Hood: Empath Maintenance

Empaths are finely tuned, sensitive instruments. Like a musical instruments, they need adequate care in order to function properly.

The person who can best take care of you is *yourself*.

You know how different situations make you feel and you know how to handle them in a way that feels good to you.

I strongly caution you against giving your power away to friends and family members by expecting them to know how to take care of you.

They don't know what's best for you, even if they are Empaths themselves. Their situation is different than yours and they might have completely different preferences than yours, both in what problems they run into and how to best solve them.

You have no control over what other people chose to do, think or feel. Oftentimes, they don't have control over it themselves! They're just reacting to life according to years of conditioning and unconscious habits.

However, you do have plenty of control over what *you* do, think and feel. This is where your power awaits you: within.

The **Empath Survival Program**© introduced you to basic techniques you can use to regain your emotional sanity and identify what's yours and what belongs to other people.

In addition to knowing how to handle every day life situations, you will also feel much better if you have a regular self-care routine to handle *emotional confusion* and *emotional fatigue.*

## Emotional Confusion

Although tools and techniques can help you manage everyday life, it's very likely that you'll find yourself in a common Empath situation at some point: emotional confusion.

Impaired Empaths practically live in this state of being: feeling lost, confused about how they feel (either in a specific situation or about life in general), uninspired to move forward, bouncing from one overwhelming situation to the next...

Having spent the first 30 years of my life this way, I'm familiar with the fact that even minor events can send us into such a tailspin. Whenever my son was sick, for example, my Empath skills would turn on full blast, in case I could pick up something useful from him about how to help him. Which would only make matters worse, as I would then feel his issues on top of mine!

The same thing can happen if you're struggling with emotionally challenging situations, such as work, money, health issues, or your love life. These situations can become triggers that accidentally push us to "tune into" other people, looking for information, until we're completely overwhelmed and stuck in even more trouble!

# Emotional Fatigue

Impaired Empaths also have a high risk of experiencing a form of emotional exhaustion, where nothing feels good anymore.

Decisional fatigue refers to the deteriorating quality of decisions made by an individual, after a long session of decision-making. This concept has been studied extensively in psychology, which has shown that people who have to make a lot of decisions as part of their daily job, like judges for example, become worn out over time and tend to make poorer choices later in the day. The mind becomes exhausted and has a hard time evaluating trade offs, a critical skill in decision-making.

In a similar vein, Empaths can become overly activated by the constant emotional information that they have to process, leading to emotional fatigue. This is especially true for Impaired Empaths who have a hard time regulating the influx of emotions they pick up from other people. Over time, their ability to appropriately respond to emotions can become erratic, leaving them feeling powerless and depressed.

Under a spell of emotional fatigue, you might start to feel sad without knowing why. You are also more likely to feel depressed later in the day, waking up fine in the morning but experiencing a decline in your positive emotions as the day goes by. The Empath blues is typically temporary but can become chronic if left unattended.

A word of caution: anyone who feels depressed over a long period of time might be suffering from clinical depression and should seek medical help as well as therapeutic counseling.

Emotions are surprisingly like food: in order to move through us, they have to be processed by a digestive system. An Empath needs to be comfortable processing three categories of problem emotions: **external**, **stagnant**, and **overpowering**.

**External Emotions** are emotions that come from other people. Although experiencing other people's emotions as our own is not a problem in itself, that state of being should always be temporary.

When it's appropriate (for example, during a counseling session), feeling external emotions can provide information, deeper meaning, and clarity about someone else's emotional experience.

**Stagnant Emotions** are emotions that are stuck in our energy, just sitting there like dead weight.

For example, if my spouse hates his job but he is the single breadwinner for the family, he might feel stuck in this emotion because he feels nothing can be done about it.

Or if a mother is utterly frustrated with a child who is struggling at school, that feeling might be stuck because she afraid to explode with anger during the emotional processing.

Being afraid of our own emotions can completely block our ability to experience and express them.

**Overpowering Emotions** are emotions that are just too big to fit within our emotional space. Intense rage, obsession, or anxiety all have the potential to turn into a huge balloon that can't be managed by our mind. What makes them difficult to process is their sheer intensity.

A Balanced Empath can handle very-high-intensity emotions without them becoming overpowering emotions. An incoming wave of rage from a co-worker does not inevitably have to mow down an Empath.

However, Empaths must pay extra attention to external, stagnant, and overpowering emotions to avoid letting them get stuck in our energy and start clumping together. That's how a small unprocessed emotion can turn into a huge ball of despair, where you can't even pinpoint why you feel so bad anymore.

## Self-Care for Empaths

Addressing emotional confusion and emotional fatigue is a self-discovery process. To this day, I still find new ways to fine-tune the way I manage my emotional space.

Even when accounting for personal differences, there seem to be common practices that are a natural fit for Empaths to resolve these problems and which should be part of your self-care routine.

## Talk to Someone

The ONE thing that really helps with emotional confusion is to *talk to someone that understands your situation.*

After years of doing this by myself, I finally reached out to a spiritual counselor (I didn't even know there was such a thing!). Being able to honestly discuss my emotional turmoil with someone who understood my Empath skills was, by far, the most effective way out of an emotional tailspin.

In the beginning, I talked to her every week. This process helped me articulate and understand my own feelings, as well as integrating what I picked up from other people into the big picture. I quickly became able to do this more on my own, until I would only call once in a while, when something really big happened.

This is the reason I always try to keep appointments available specifically for my Empath clients, in my work as a professional intuitive. I feel it's life changing to be able to talk to someone about what's really happening to you, without having to hide important details, like the fact that you can feel other people's emotions!

There is nothing more comforting than talking honestly with someone who will not think you're weird, and who understands what is really going on.

I am often the only person in my client's life with whom they can talk *authentically*. And they usually have waited for years, sometimes decades, before reaching out to someone.

No matter how you get it (counselor, friend, web site, etc.), it is vitally important to receive *support*. Trying to do this on your own is one more hurdle you have to jump before you can finally make sense of what is happening. If you have not done so already, please reach out to someone to get help when you need it!

I am always delighted to work with Empaths and you can register for a session with me here: http://www.EliseLebeau.com/help.

## Being alone

Empaths need time by themselves when they are less likely to be tuning into the emotions of others around them. It doesn't mean you're anti-social or that you don't like people! It just means you need to refuel before going back out into the world.

Make sure you have plenty of alone time during which you're doing something that is not emotional, such as knitting, gardening, or cooking. I like to play video games, which is mentally engaging but has no emotional triggers for me. Be creative!

## Being in nature

Many Empaths report feeling most at peace in nature: among trees, near mountains, and in large bodies of water such as the ocean or a lake. And for good reasons! Trees and water provide a natural "white noise" when it comes to emotional energy. It's like wearing a noise-cancelling headset to drown out the emotions of other people. I walk several miles a week in the forest around my house, which rejuvenates and energizes me for the day.

## Being physically active

Physical activity can provide a great buffer against emotional fatigue by taking our focus away from ours emotions and into our physical body, giving us some emotional breathing space.

It can also help to release stagnant emotions. You might find yourself weeping uncontrollably after a good run. That's ok! The physical activity has stirred up your energy and gotten those tricky emotions unblocked.

The physical activity needs to be challenging enough that it requires your full attention. Rock climbing and yoga are my favorites.

## Meditation

Meditation can provide a gentle way to guide your focus away from other people. This can be very challenging for Empaths who tend to always want to tune into others. It might feel unnatural or difficult at first. It took me well over a year to find meditations that I enjoyed.

But being able to create a quiet space within, whether by focusing on your breath or by following a guided audio meditation, can give you the space you need to rest both your mind and your sensitive emotional system. Even a five-minute meditation can improve the way you react to your day, no matter how challenging it turns out to be.

# The Empath Hypothesis: Emerging Science

## The Biology of Empaths

Although you probably have an *intuitive understanding* of your Empath skills, it's important to have *intellectual knowledge* as well. It's easier for the brain to accept something that it can explain.

Everyone is born an Empath. We all have the physical *equipment* necessary to pick up on what other people feel. But, for most of us, this ability will fade away from lack of use. To see how this works, let's look into the physiological processes involved.

When you *think* about something, it triggers electrical activity in your brain. A very mild electric current will activate neurons (special cells that relay information in the body). These neurons then activate other neurons, and create a chain reaction.

Each thought triggers a unique pattern in the brain, called a *neuron pathway*. Scientists already know that the neuron pathway varies with the type of intellectual activity you're doing. For example, when language is involved, Broca's area (located behind your left temple) will get electrically stimulated.

All this electrical activity generates a *magnetic field* (which is true for all electrical currents). As Empaths, we are able to read and interpret this magnetic information. Our own brain translates these magnetic patterns into an emotion that we personally experience.

Think of it like having a portable MRI machine (Magnetic Resonance Imaging) in your brain. You can "take pictures" of magnetic waves and translate them into something meaningful. Doctors use MRI scans to differentiate between sick and healthy cells. We use it to differentiate between emotional states.

## Reading Magnetic Information

When someone is angry, all kinds of electrical and chemical reactions happening in their body (sweating, getting flustered, faster heart beat). All these changes trigger mild electrical currents that create a magnetic field around their physical body.

As an Empath, you can sense this magnetic information and "read" their state of mind: this person is angry. Although the pattern changes from one person to the next, Empaths are able to interpret and "translate" it to an emotion they personally experience.

## Mirror Neurons

Things can looks like magic until we figure out how they work and understand the processes involved.

Unfortunately for Empaths, this discovery is still underway. However, research on mirror neurons is finally shedding some light on a potential explanation for the way Empaths experience the emotions of others.

Mirror neurons are thought to be a neurophysiological mechanism involved in how we understand the actions of others and learn to imitate them (Rizzolatti and Craighero 169-192).

These neurons were first studied in the context of motor skills and were observed to fire up when a monkey was watching someone else perform an action.

This led to the hypothesis that watching others do something triggers an internal response that can help us mimic and imitate what we see. The very act of watching another experiencing something activates neurons in our own brain, even when we are not personally performing the action (Bastiaansen, Thioux and Keysers 2391-2404).

In his ground breaking book, *Mirroring People*, Marco Iacoboni relates the evolution of this fascinating new field of research. He introduces mirror neurons as the potential physiological basis for empathy and morality, since they seem to be involved in how we can perceive and interpret the experiences of other people (Iacoboni 4).

In its simplest form, a mirror neuron is triggered by the observation of a physical gesture in someone else, which in turns fires the same physiological neurons in the observer. What is striking about this process is that it happens consistently even though the observer does not move his muscles at all. It's only an internal representation of the action, not a physical imitation of it.

Taking the example of a baseball game, the neurons activated by the catcher as he grabs the ball also get fired in the audience as they watch him do it. The same process is also at work when we watch someone experiencing physical pain or notice facial expression of anger or worry. Our brain can interpret the meaning of all these situations by internally experiencing them through its own mirror neurons.

Not only that, but there is a plethora of ways to trigger the mirror neurons: watching a ball being kicked, hearing the sound of a ball being kicked or even just saying the word "kick", can all fire up the mirror neurons involved in this activity.

There is also a very high level of sophistication in the mirror neurons' firing pattern. In fact, the pattern is specific to the context or meaning of the action being observed, such as raising your hand to grab a ball or raising your hand to ask a question. These two actions involve the same muscle, but not the same intention, and they trigger different mirror neuron pathways.

In short, mirror neurons allow us to create a very specific, contextual internal representation of what others are experiencing by firing our own brain cells to bring meaning and understanding to the actions of others.

This leads Iacoboni to postulate that the firing pattern of mirror neurons is actually complex enough that it allows us to understand the intention of other people (i.e. "what they are thinking") depending on the context of their action (Iacoboni 30).

The presence of this biological process is critical when you consider that being able to understand and relate to other people is critical in our ability to survive in human society.

## The Sensitive Empath

That concept of sensitivity is central to the Empath Experience. Empaths report feeling very stirred by what they watch or read, such as a sad movie. They tend to avoid watching the news as the simple act of listening to someone else's story of disaster triggers the very same perturbing emotions within them.

Empaths who listen to their friend talk about a distressing situation report still feeling negative emotions long after the conversation is over.

Since negative emotions are more salient and noticeable, most Empaths report feeling the weight of the world on their shoulders, as these emotions keep piling up.

As such, Empaths are often described as overly sensitive people, through their own self-evaluation and the observation of their family and friends. This is not surprising considering that Empaths are constantly feeling some form of emotion, whether it is their own or not. They are constantly emotionally activated, which can make them look overly sensitive.

But that sensitivity might go further than just being especially vulnerable to tear jerker commercials. They might also have a more sensitive nervous system.

Research shows that some people are naturally more sensitive than others. Even young babies exhibit differences in the way they respond to unfamiliar events (Kagan 139-143).

In a large study of 462 healthy subjects, Kagan found that about 20% of these children were more reactive and became more distressed when exposed to unfamiliar visual, auditory, and tactile stimulations. These sensitive children might grow up to become emotionally sensitive adults as well.

The term "highly sensitive person" has also been used to describe people who react strongly to life's situations. Dr. Elaine Aron has been a powerful advocate for the concept that being sensitive is a personality trait more complex than the introverted/extroverted Jungian concepts (Aron 6).

As described by Kagan, certain people have a natural sensitivity from birth, which makes it more difficult for them to be comfortable. Our bodies and minds naturally seek to find a happy medium between boredom and over-stimulation.

Being highly sensitive can be challenging since the world itself quickly becomes overwhelming.

Bright lights, loud noises, strong colors or odors, all these stimuli can overrun a delicate nervous system until nothing feels good and there is no peace to be had.

Most importantly, Aron is adamant that being highly sensitive is a gift, a skill, a talent that should be praised and appreciated instead of criticized and ridiculed. She hopes that once highly sensitive people understand why they react the way they do when they are over-stimulated, things will make sense, they can finally understand themselves better, and, hopefully, accept themselves as they are.

This is a major divergence from the "what's wrong with you" mentality that surrounds most sensitive people since childhood. Parents despair as their child cries endlessly, friends don't understand sudden needs to withdraw to be alone, and teachers are exasperated by what seems to be a deep lack of attention to the tasks at hand.

Yet, all these can be explained by an overwhelmed nervous system, along with relatively simple solutions to address the situation in order to bring balance into a frazzled mind and an overloaded body.

Just like some people have better hearing or vision, Empaths might have a more acute sensitivity to emotional signals. They could be a sort of "natural antenna" for this kind of information that somehow reads and interprets external emotions while others would feel nothing at all.

The biological apparatus is there for everyone, but for Empaths the signal is always on, always loud, and usually disruptive.

The concepts of mirror neurons and emotional contagion also support the view that humans might be biologically equipped to perceive the emotions of another person, but that Empaths simply have a more sensitive receptivity for these signals.

However, there is an aspect of the Empath experience that goes beyond what has been explored so far by researchers. Empaths report being able to perceive other people's emotions even when they are not in their physical presence, often across very large distances.

This means that the emotional stimuli is not visual (seeing someone's facial expression), auditory (hearing a baby cry) or tactile (feeling the bodily spasms of sobbing).

Some Empaths report being affected by the emotions of their family and friends who live hundreds or thousands of miles away.

However unbelievable, the process involved in such a feat could be relatively simple. If specific emotions trigger very specialized neuronal pathways, the magnetic field generated by this electrical activity might be picked up by someone else's mirror neurons, triggering emotional contagion.

If we think of person A as being the emitter and person B as being the receiver, both parties possess the biological equipment necessary to "send" and "receive" emotional signals. Person A is automatically transmitting a magnetic field that reflects the electrical activity associated with their emotional activation, much like the images of an MRI (Magnetic Resonance Imaging) reflects the internal activities of the brain.

Meanwhile, person B could receive and interpret this magnetic activity through their mirror neurons, providing them with a personal experience of person A's emotional state.

This mechanism could explain why Empaths can feel the emotions of people who are not in their physical presence.

Contrary to electrical current which needs a conductive substance in order to travel, magnetic waves can go through solids and keep traveling great distances with minimal (or theoretically non-existent) loss. An MRI can digitalize pictures of soft tissue located inside of the skull because of this property.

As such, the magnetic field emitted by a person, albeit extremely faint and complex, can travel unaltered indefinitely. Electro-sensitivity (i.e. the ability to feel electro-magnetic fields) is highly controversial and often deemed inexistent, but its presence has been postulated as theoretical.

What would it take for this process to work? First, person A would have to experience an emotion that is strong and specific enough to emit a signal that can be read and interpreted by person B. This is highly consistent with the Empath experience, where people report being overwhelmed primarily by strong negative emotions such as anger and depression. They also say that the emotions they pick up from others stay with them longer when the emotion is very strong.

Second, person B would have to be sensitive enough to be able to perceive this faint magnetic field and isolate it from every other bit of magnetic information that constantly surrounds us. Indeed, this is where Empaths seem to be different from people who do not have Empath experiences: they are always described as "overly sensitive".

In everyday life, that usually means people who constantly experience emotions more frequently and deeply than others. In our scenario, person B would have to be not only sensitive enough to differentiate this emotional signal from that from a microwave for example, but also be versed enough in emotional content to contextually identify which emotion is being perceived (like anger).

That seems like a lot of very complex, specialized information which is unlikely to be processed consciously. On the contrary, Empaths report having these emotional experiences without meaning to do so, thus indicating that the process is more likely to be biological instead of cognitive.

If we go back to the hypothesis that mirror neurons could be the physiological process by which we can feel what other people feel, this process could be happening unconsciously where similar mirror neurons would be triggered within person B, thus offering very specific contextual information as to what emotion person A is experiencing. The experience of anger in person A could fire mirror neurons in person B, assuming that person is an Empath.

This process corresponds to how Empaths describe their experience (feel first, think later) as well as being in line with Iacoboni suggestion that mirror neurons could be heavily involved in the psychological process of empathy (Iacoboni 12).

This is different from more-traditional psychological perspectives where the processing of emotions is considered to be mostly cognitive. And yet, there are some fundamental commonalities between the Empath experience and the more cognitive term of "empathy" which has been extensively studied in psychology.

# The Psychology of Empaths

## Empath or Empathy?

Empathy is a concept widely used in psychology to define the ability to imagine what another person is feeling, colloquially known as "walking in someone else's shoes". It plays a crucial role in our social interactions. Feeling empathy towards someone else may alter how we act towards them. For example, empathy might lead us to hug someone who is crying from emotional distress. It's an intricate part of the glue that holds human beings together as a society.

Theodore Lipps is considered the father of the term empathy (Montag, Gallinat and Heinz 1261). He used it to describe how we perceive the mental state of others by a process of inner imitation. This internal process involves several areas of the brain, such as the cortex, the autonomic nervous system, the hypothalamic-pituitary-adrenal axis and endocrine system (J. Decety 92-108).

Although people who suffer from some psychopathologies, such sociopaths, can exhibit a lack of empathy, this ability has a strong biological basis. Babies can recognize different emotions very early in life and toddlers develop their sense for empathy as they mature. Young children are not only able to identify the emotions of others but they can also interpret them appropriately.

For example, a child who sees another child get hurt and cry might walk over to offer his blanket as comfort.

Carl Rogers defined empathy as the ability to "perceive the internal frame of reference of another with accuracy and with the emotional components and meanings which pertain thereto as if one were the person, but without ever losing the 'as if' conditions" (Rogers 210-211).

By this, he means that empathy is an imaginary process by which we hypothesize about the emotions of others "as if" it was happening to us.

Recent evidence describes two different system involved in the process of psychological empathy: an emotion based contagion system, meaning "I feel what you feel" and a more cognitive perspective-taking system, meaning "I understand what you feel" (Shamay-Tsoory, Aharon-Peretz and Perry 617-627).

The emotional empathy process seems to activate the inferior frontal gyrus while the cognitive empathy process is more closely tied to the motor mirror neuron system. The model described by Rogers seems to be more related to cognitive empathy than emotional empathy.

Since the Empath experience involves mostly emotions, it seems more related to emotional empathy. However, the Empath experience might be unique in the sense that even the most basic form of psychological empathy is always deemed to involve cognitive aspects (Shamay-Tsoory, Aharon-Peretz and Perry 617-627).

But for empaths, what they feel is first and foremost. Thus, there are several critical aspects involved in the psychological understanding of empathy, which are fundamentally different from the Empath experience.

First, in order to "perceive the internal frame of reference of another" as Rogers describes, one must have a mental experience of the other person.

Most psychological experiments that study empathy use observation as a means to trigger empathy, where children or adults are made to watch someone who is put in a situation meant to elicit strong emotions. Such situations could involve being mistreated (for negative emotions) or receiving a gift (for positive emotions).

Empathy might also be triggered by hearing sounds (such as a baby crying) or interacting with someone as they relate an emotionally charged personal experience. The common thread being that all these situations require a direct contact with the target in order to trigger empathy.

This is drastically different from the Empath experience. Empaths often report feeling the emotions of people who are not in their physical presence and with whom they've had no contact (Jude) (Lebeau, What is an Empath?).

For example, they might experience a strong emotion just as they are about to enter a room where someone is crying; as they pick up a phone call from a loved one who is distressed by bad news; as they walk through a hospital where patient are in physical pain.

The Empath experience does not rely on visual or auditory cues, nor does it require a mental representation of the person whose emotions are being perceived.  On the contrary, it is a direct emotional connection to their internal emotional state that is not triggered by a mental representation.

Second, Rogers emphasizes that empathy involves an "as if" condition. One might experience empathy when they can imagine what the other person feels like as if it were happening to them.

This is very different for the Empath experience. Empaths feel other people's emotions as their own, not as being imagined or coming from an external source.

As they pick up the phone for call from someone who is distressed with bad news, they might experience a profound sense of dread or sadness, without knowing why.

The Empath experience goes deeper than just a mental representation of another's emotional experience. It's a personal direct experience, often both physical and emotional.

Most fundamentally, empathy and the Empath experience differ in the following way: the trigger to empathy is an external cue, such as a negative facial expression, while the trigger to the Empath experience is an internal cue, such as a change in one's own emotional state.

Empathy involves thinking first, then feeling. The Empath experience involves feeling first, then thinking.

Unfortunately, many Empaths do not know how to process this external emotional experience, which can lead to a confusing situation where both types of emotions become entangled and thus extremely difficult to differentiate.

In fact, most Empaths experience mild to severe emotional distress from their experiences. It is often called the "Empath curse" (Brallier), describing the emotional trauma that comes from experiencing all the negative emotions of everyone around you, without being able to identify which ones are yours and which ones belong to other people.

This can lead to great emotional distress and mental strain.

The problem is compounded by the fact that most Empaths do not realize what is happening to them. The aberrant changes in their emotional state are often attributed to depression or other mental health issues, since they cannot be directly related to their immediate life circumstances.

For example, if their neighbor is grieving for the death of his wife, an Empath might experience an intense sense of depression and loss, which has nothing to do with their own situation. This can lead to complicated issues where an Empath is being treated for someone else problem.

Finally, empathy and the Empath experience also differ in how they are subjectively perceived. While empathy is seen as being a positive quality that parents aspire to teach their children, the Empath experience is often perceived as chaotic and painful. This situation is mostly attributable to the fact that little is known about the Empath experience and most people go through it unconsciously.

They do not realize what is happening to them nor do they know how to control the influx of external emotions that is flooding their consciousness.

Unlike people who are experiencing empathy, Empaths are unable to differentiate the feelings of others from their own. In their early years, Empath children report experiencing all kinds of emotions, usually negative in nature, that they interpret feel as being their own, even when there are no immediate circumstances that could explain these feelings. For example, they might swing from feeling completely depressed to violently angry with no obvious reason.

Even as adults, Empaths often experience years of incomprehensible emotional turmoil before finally considering the impossible: that somehow they can pick up emotions that are not theirs.

This is where the concept of emotional transmission through mirror neurons comes in to fill the gap. If we consider that the trigger for an Empath experience might be a *physical event* where the magnetic field emitted by someone else's emotion triggers an empath's mirror neurons, it starts to make sense.

The Empath would feel first, and then try to understand what they are feeling. The trigger being both internal and yet caused by external event would likely cause great confusion as to what is happening. It could easily lead to a profound desire to shut it down and remain in denial out of sheer frustration. Indeed, this is the process described by so many Empaths.

# Why are we Empaths?

After the awakening, understanding and acceptance of being an Empath, we can step into a deeper spiritual experience that awaits us. Instead of being a helpless spectator in the suffering of others, we become inspired to express what we feel in a way that empowers and heals.

This can manifest in an infinite number of ways, through artwork, emotionally authentic psychotherapy or the integration of the Empath experiences in everyday life.

Being able to connect through emotions is a direct link between two people's inner being. It has the potential to bring authenticity and spiritual depth to everyday life.

Ultimately, the meaning of the Empath experience is not an external pursuit. In fact, Balanced Empaths report using their skill in their existing life, no matter what they do for a living.

The calling of an Empath only requires emotional authenticity, something that comes naturally to us. From there, every interaction becomes charged with spiritual meaning by the very act of connecting to others authentically. Empaths can feel empowered by their contribution to every life they touch, through every emotion they express.

From a very young age, human beings seek connections to other people.  We're not a solitary race. From parents to friends, we spend a huge amount of energy trying to develop meaningful relationships with the people around us.

And yet establishing these connections can be very challenging. A quick glance at the number of books published on the topic of relationships easily conveys how difficult it can be to communicate authentically with other people.

This is especially true in our Western culture where so many social conventions actively discourage people from being authentic.

For example, lying about not liking someone "to be polite" or concealing feelings of anger because it's "not feminine". There's a plethora of reasons why people hide their feelings, which has led us to struggle when we want to relate to other people because we don't know how they really feel.

Authenticity is been weeded out of us and Empaths feel this most acutely. Every dishonest, misleading and manipulative conversation feels like screeching nails on a chalkboard. We can't always tell why we're irked but we can tell something is amiss.

There's something profoundly unnatural in the act of disconnecting from our own feelings. All we're left with are tenuous social contracts, often based on obligation or self-interest, which push us farther way from each other.

It might not be that surprising that Empaths would surface in our society.

They bring the ability to be empathically accurate (Mast, Ickes and Farrow 408-427), meaning that they can tell what another person is feeling, even when it is not perceivable through verbal or nonverbal cues.

They can connect to other people's true feelings. Even though most humans don't consider themselves part of nature anymore, nature still affect us and, most importantly, tries to keep us in balance.

Empaths have an inner sense that they are some sort healer of emotions. Of course, being aware of another person's feeling does not mean we can fix the situation. But it does offer a unique opportunity to open a sensitive dialogue about what is really going on.

An Empath brings empathy and authenticity to every day life and everyone they encounter. It is their gift to our world.

# References

Aron, Elaine N. *The Highly Sensitive Person*. New
York: Broadway Books, 1997. Print.

Bastiaansen, J, M Thioux and C Keysers. "Evidence for
mirror systems in emotions." *Philosophical
Transactions of the Royal Society of London - Series B:
Biological Sciences* 2009: 2391-2404. Print.

Brallier, Sylvia. *The Joys and Pitfalls of Being an
Empath*. n.d. 27 December 2011. <http://
healing.about.com/od/empathic/a/
empathessential.htm>.

Chartrand, Tanya L, and John A Bargh. "The chameleon
effect: the perception-behavior link and social
interaction." *Journal of Personality and Social
Psychology* 76.6 (1999): 893-910. Print.

Decety, J and P L Jackson. "The architecture of human empathy." *Behavioral and Cognitive Neuroscience Reviews* 3.2 (2004): 71-100. Print.

Decety, Jean. "Dissecting the Neural Mechanisms Mediating Empathy." *Emotion Review* 2011: 92-108. Print.

Iacoboni, Marco. *Mirroring People*. New York: Farrar, Straus and Giroux, 2008. Print.

Jude, Nick. *The Empath Guide*. n.d. Web. 19 December 2011. <http://www.empathguide.com/>.

Kagan, Jerome. "Temperament and the Reactions to Unfamiliarity." *Child Development* 1997: 139-143.

Lebeau, Elise. *The Empath Community*. 17 November
2007. Web. <http://
EmpathCommunity.EliseLebeau.com>.


Lebeau, Elise. *What is an Empath?* 30 April 2008.
Web. <http://www.EliseLebeau.com/empaths>.


Lebeau, Elise. *The Empath Survival Program*.
February 2008. Web. <http://www.EliseLebeau.com/
empath-survival-program>.


Mast, Marianne Schmid, et al. *Empathy in mental
illness*. Cambridge University Press, 2007. Print.


Meltzoff, A N, and M K Moore. "Newborn infants
imitate adult facial gestures." *Child Development* 54.3
(1983): 702-709. Print.

Montag, Christiane, Jurgen Gallinat and Andreas Heinz. "Theodor Lipps and the concept of empathy: 1851-1914." *The American Journal of Psychiatry* 2008: 1261. Print.

Rizzolatti, Giacomo and Laila Craighero. "The Mirror Neuron System." *Annual Review of Neuroscience* 2004: 169-192.

Rogers, Carl. "A theory of therapy, personality, and interpersonal relationships, as developed in the client-centered framework." 1959: 184-256. Print.

Schoenewolf, Gerald. "Emotional Contagion: Behavioral induction in individuals and groups." *Modern Psychoanalysis* 15.1 (1990): 49-61. Print.

Shamay-Tsoory, Simone G, Judith Aharon-Peretz and Daniella Perry. "Two systems for empathy: a double dissociation." *Brain: A journal of neurology* 132.Pt 3 (2009): 617-627. Print.

Made in the USA
Middletown, DE
05 August 2018